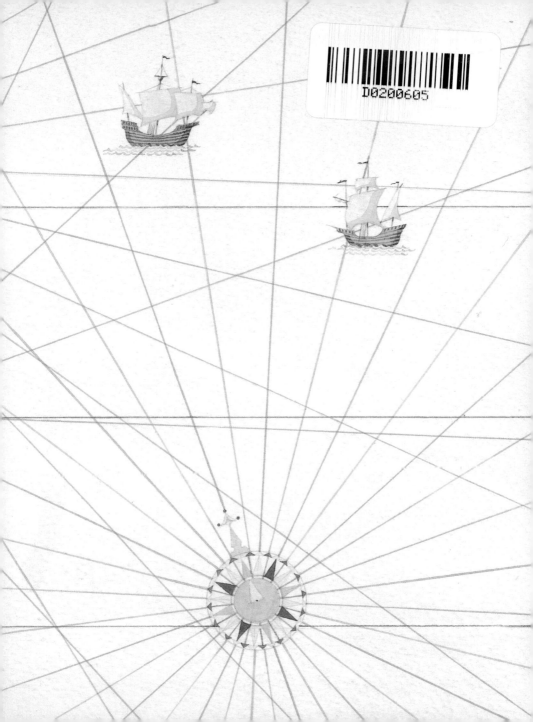

Off the Beaten Path

Off the Beaten Path

A TRAVELER'S ANTHOLOGY

LAURA STODDART

CHRONICLE BOOKS

SAN FRANCISCO

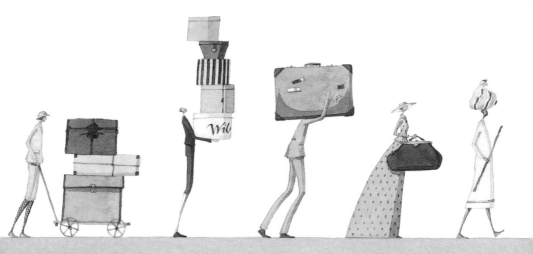

To my own traveller
J.D.C.

First published in the United States in 2003 by Chronicle Books LLC

Illustrations and text selection copyright © 2003 by Laura Stoddart

Researched by Jane Fior and Camilla Stoddart

Library of Congress Cataloging-in-Publication Data available upon request.

ISBN: 0-8118-3775-0

Manufactued in Italy

10 9 8 7 6 5 4 3 2 1

Chronicle Books LLC
85 Second Street
San Francisco, California 94105

www.chroniclebooks.com

CONTENTS

Who seeks the way to win renown,
Or flies with wings of high desire,
Who seeks to wear the laurel crown,
Or hath the mind that would aspire,
Let him his native soil eschew,
Let him go range and seek a new.

Sir Richard Grenville (c. 1541–1591) from
'In Praise of Seafaring Men, in Hopes of
Good Fortune'

In Search of Adventure

PART I

Qualifications for a Traveller: If you have health, a great craving for adventure, at least a moderate fortune, and can set your heart on a definite object, which old travellers do not think impracticable, then — travel by all means. If, in addition to these qualifications, you have scientific taste and knowledge, I believe that no career, in time of peace, can offer to you more advantages than that of a traveller.

Francis Galton from *The Art of Travel*, 1855

Since life is short and the world is wide, the sooner you start exploring it the better.

Simon Raven from an article in *The Spectator*, 1968

I was not born for one corner; the whole world is my native land.

Lucius Annaeus Seneca (c. 4 B.C. – c. A.D. 65)

Once more on my adventure brave and new.
Robert Browning (1812–1889) from 'Rabbi Ben Ezra'

A wanderer is man from his birth
He was born in a ship
On the breast of the river of Time.

Matthew Arnold (1822–1888) from 'The Future'

Beyond the East the sunrise,
beyond the West the sea,
And East and West the wander-thirst
that will not let me be.

Gerald Gould from 'Wander-Thirst'

I want to go wandering. Who shall declare
I will regret if I dare?

Vachel Lindsay from 'I want to go Wandering', 1904

The true wanderer, whose travels are happiness, goes out not to
shun, but to seek.

Freya Stark (1893–1993) from an article in *The Spectator*, 1950

TERRA INCOGNITA

Be let that man with better sense of advize
That of the world least part to us is red;
And daily how through hardy enterprize
Many great regions are discovered.

Edmund Spenser (1522–1599) from *The Faerie Queen*

It is the opinion of Plancius and other geographers that there are
no other lands which have not yet been discovered and which
God may be reserving for the glory and advantage of other
princes …

Pierre Jeannin, Ambassador to King Henry IV of France, 1605

I resolved to abandon trade, and to fix my aim on something
more praiseworthy and stable: whence it was that I made
preparation for going to see part of the world and its wonders.

Amerigo Vespucci (1451–1512) from his 'Letter concerning the Isles Newly
Discovered' in *Four Voyages*

Were it not for the pleasure which naturally results to a man from
being the first discoverer, even of nothing more than sand and
shoals, this service would be insupportable, especially in far
distant parts like this, short of provisions and almost every other
necessity. The world will hardly admit of an excuse for a man
leaving a coast unexplored he has once discovered.

Captain James Cook (1728–1779) from his own log and journals,
17 August 1770

13

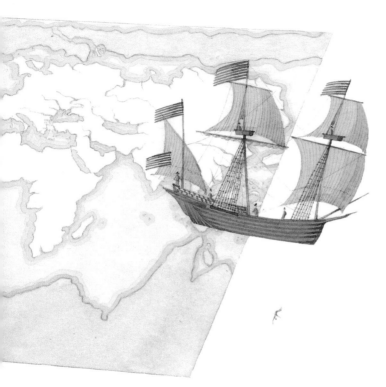

They are ill discoverers that think there is no land, when they can see nothing but sea.

Francis Bacon (1561–1625) from *The Advancement of Learning*

For my own part, I cannot but think it exceedingly ridiculous to hear some men talk of the circumference of the earth, pretending, without the smallest reason of probability, that the ocean encompasses the earth, that the earth is round, as if mechanically formed so.

Herodotus (c. 485–425 B.C.)

I have come to another conclusion respecting the earth, namely that it is not round as they describe, but of the form of a pear, which is very round except where the stalk grows, at which part it is most prominent.

Christopher Columbus (1451–1506) from *The History of a Voyage which Don Christopher Columbus Made the Third Time He Came to the Indies, When He Discovered Terra Firma*

'I quite realised,' said Columbus,
'That the earth was not a rhombus,
But I am a little annoyed
To find it a oblate spheroid.'

E Clerihew Bentley (1875–1956) from *More Biography*

Map me no maps, sir, my head is a map, a map of the whole world.

Henry Fielding (1707–1754) from *Rape Upon Rape*

It is not down in any map, true places never are.

Herman Melville (1819–1891) from *Moby Dick*

When the inspiration for walking and tramping has come we realise what a boon maps are, we come to love them, as inseparable companions. You put local maps of countries and towns and countrysides in your pockets, and large folded maps of the Continent in your knapsacks. You unfold them in the desert; you lie on them, you crawl about with a magnifying glass examining their small print and the lost names of villages in smudged mountain-ranges … You survey with a curious joy the dotted line of your peregrinations up to that point.

Stephen Graham from *The Gentle Art of Tramping*, 1927

Biography is about chaps;
Geography is about maps.

Anonymous

Advice to the Traveler

PART II

Farewell Monsieur Traveller: look you lisp and wear strange suits, disable all the benefits of your own country, be out of love with your nativity, and almost chide God for making you that countenance you are, or I will scarce think you have swam in a gondola.

William Shakespeare (1564–1616) from *As You Like It*

Patience, tact and abundance of time are necessary, and the would-be traveller lacking in any of these essentials should seek lands where less primitive methods obtain.

Ernest Henry Wilson (1876–1930) from *A Naturalist in Western China*, 1913

I told him I intended going to West Africa and he said 'When you have made up your mind to go to West Africa the very best thing you can do, is to get it unmade again and go to Scotland instead; but if your intelligence is not strong enough to do so … get some introductions to the Weslyans: they are the only people on the Coast who have got a hearse with feathers.'

Mary Kingsley (1862–1900) from *Travels in West Africa*, 1897

The importance of flannel next to the skin can hardly be overrated: it is now a matter of statistics; for, during the progress of expeditions, notes have been made of the number of names of those in them who had provided themselves with flannel, and of those who had not.

Francis Galton from *The Art of Travel* (1872)

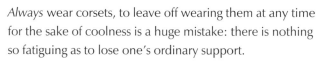

Always wear corsets, to leave off wearing them at any time for the sake of coolness is a huge mistake: there is nothing so fatiguing as to lose one's ordinary support.

Constance Larymore from *A Resident's Wife in Nigeria*, 1908

The roads are steep and dangerous, the cold wind is extremely biting, and frequently fierce dragons impede and molest travellers with their inflictions. Those who travel this road should not wear red garments nor carry loud-sounding calabashes.

Hsuan Tsang (645–664) from *Dangers of Travel in the Mountains*

I was so ill provided with the clothing necessary for this latitude that I was a little pinched by the frost, though I put on my whole wardrobe at once, that is two pairs of breeches, two pairs of worsted stockings and fur boots upon them, two pairs of gloves, two coats, two waistcoats, a greatcoat and a cloak overall and yet I sat shivering.

Reginald Pole Carew (1753–1835) in a letter to the Earl of Crawford, 1781

A powder bag made out of a woman's glove.

A razor.

Thread.

Needles.

Scissors.

A comb, carried in one pair of dress shoes.

A pair of silk stockings.

Breeches, fine enough, when folded, not bigger than a fist.

Two very fine shirts.

Three cravats.

Three handkerchiefs.

The clothes in which I travelled.

Chevalier de la Tocnaye from *A Frenchman's Walk through Ireland* (1796–1797)

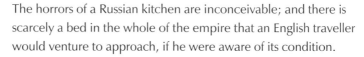

The horrors of a Russian kitchen are inconceivable; and there is scarcely a bed in the whole of the empire that an English traveller would venture to approach, if he were aware of its condition.

E D Clarke from *Travels in Various Countries*

I hardly remember one place where some of us did not sleep in the same room in which we supped — for it was generally furnished with two or three beds and those beds almost as generally occupied with troops of bugs, and whole armies of fleas. The nightly excursions and attacks of those hopping and creeping gentry were a great annoyance to all the company except myself, who happily have not the honour of being to their great taste.

Walter Stanhope from a letter to his mother, 11 July 1769

Clean straw and fair Water are blessings not allways to be found and better Accommodation not to be hop'd. Tho I carry my own bed with me, I could not sometimes find a place to set it up in, and I rather chose to travel all night, as cold as it is, wrap'd up in my furs, than go into the common Stoves, which are fill'd with a mixture of all sorts of ill Scents.

Lady Mary Wortley Montagu (1689–1792) from a letter to Lady Mar in Bohemia

You make a German sicke, if you lay him upon a matrass, as you distemper an Italian upon a featherbed and French man to lay him in a bed without curtaines, or lodge him in a chamber without fire.

Montaigne (1533–1592) from *Essays*

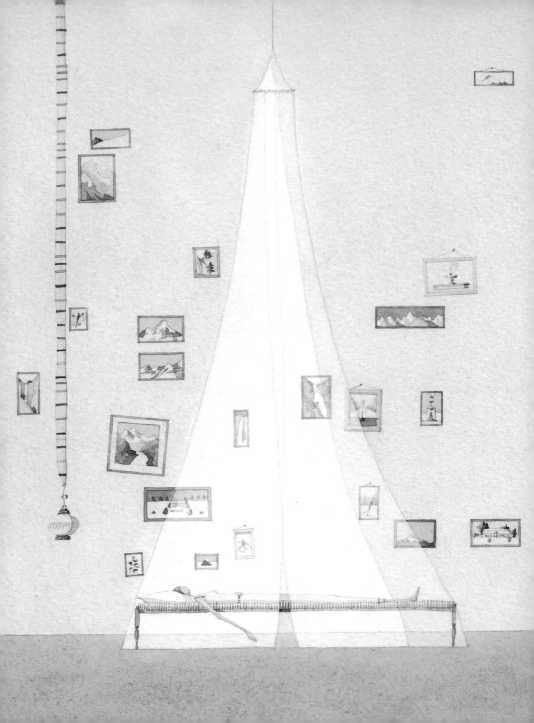

Always put up pictures of waterfalls or snow scenes —
it keeps one cool.

Constance Larymore from *A Resident's Wife in Nigeria*, 1908

Keep moving! Steam, or Gas or Stage,
Hold, cabin, steerage, hencoop's cage —
Tour, Journey, Voyage, Lounge, Ride, Walk,
Skim, Sketch, Excursion, Travel-talk —
For move you must! 'Tis now the rage,
The law and fashion of the Age.

Samuel Taylor Coleridge (1772–1834)
from 'The Delinquent Travellers'

Sooner or later the traveller must dispense with the comforts and luxuries of modern accidental methods of travel and adapt himself to those more primitive and decidedly less comfortable of the Oriental.

Ernest Henry Wilson from *A Naturalist in Western China*

The latter part of the journey I performed on elephants during the heat of the day; and a more uncomfortable mode of conveyance surely never was adopted.

Sir Joseph Dalton Hooker (1817–1911) from *Himalayan Journals*, 1848

My travelling will be slow, as I go on horseback; I find it much the best way of getting through this country for a man who has no carriage of his own; and beyond all comparison the most agreeable.

Captain John Barker in Germany, 1792

In the out-of-the-way parts of China … a chair is of greater service and value to the traveller than the passport.

Ernest Henry Wilson from *A Naturalist in Western China*

Roaming about with a good tent, and a good Arab, one
might be happy forever in India.

Fanny Parks, from Wanderings of a Pilgrim, in search of the Picturesque,
during four-and-twenty years in the East, with revelations of life in the
Zenana, *1850*

Travels in Arabia in the best circumstances, with a train of servants, good riding-beasts, tents, and your own kitchen, is a trying experience.

T E Lawrence (1888–1935) from the introduction to *Travels in Arabia Deserta* by Charles M. Doughty

There is no place where a wife is so much wanted as in the Tropics; but then comes the rub — how to keep the wife alive.

Richard Burton (1821–1890) from *Wanderings in West Africa*

35

Those Who Choose to Roam

PART III

Harkhuf

Herodotus

Alexander the Great

Pytheas

Fa Hsein

Erik the Red

Marco Polo

Henry the Navigator

Christopher Columbus

Vasco da Gama

Ferdinand Magellan

Amerigo Vespucci

Hernán Cortés

Francisco Pizarro

Giovanni de Verrazzano

Sir. Francis Drake

Sir. Walter Raleigh

Samuel de Champlain

Abel Tasman (ia)

Rene Robert Cavalier Sieur de la Salle

William Dampier

Lady Mary Wortley Montagu

Carl Linnaeus

Captain Cook

Sir. Joseph Banks

George Vancouver

Matthew Flinders

The Lander Brothers

Dr. Livingstone (I presume)

Ludwig Leichhardt

Sir. Richard Burton

John Hanning Speke

Burke and Wills

Alexandra David-Neel

Adolf Nordenskiold

Isabella Bird

Mary Kingsley

Freya Stark

Captain Scott

Ernest Shackleton

Roald Amundsen

Edmund Hillary and Sherpa Tenzing

Thor Heyerdahl

One of the pleasantest things in the world is going on a journey; but I like to go by myself.

William Hazlitt (1778–1830) from *On Going a Journey*, 1822

He who travels fastest travels alone.

Rudyard Kipling (1865–1936) from *The Winners*

Never did I think so much, exist so vividly, and experience so much as in the journeys I have taken alone and on foot.

Jean-Jacques Rousseau (1712–1778) from *Confessions*

It is usually assumed that the traveller who prefers lonely places, the desert traveller so to say, is one who wishes to escape from his world and his fellows.

Freya Stark (1893–1993) from 'The Philosophy of Travel,' *The Spectator*, 24 March 1950

The trouble with many travellers is that they take themselves along.

John Prescott from *Aphorisms and Other Observations*

I should not feel confident in venturing on a journey in a foreign country without a companion. I should want at intervals to hear the sound of my own language.

William Hazlitt from *On Going a Journey*

I believe I was born under a roaming star, and I must say, I infinitely preferred this ... way of life, unshackled as it was, to the artificial stupidity of civilisation.

Mrs Colonel Elwood from *Narrative of a Journey Overland from England*, 1830

I had been civilised all my life, and now I had a sense of freedom and expansion which quickened the blood and made the pulse beat high.

Ella Sykes from *Through Persia on a Side-Saddle*, 1898

If I were a man, I would be Richard Burton, but being only a woman, I would be Richard Burton's wife ... I long to rush around the world in an express; I feel as if I shall go mad if I remain at home.

Isabel Burton (1831–1896) from *The Inner Life of Syria, Palestine, and the Holy Land: from my Private Journal*

How I love this life in the wilderness! I shall never be content to vegetate in England.

Fanny Parks, from *Wanderings of a Pilgrim*, 1850

I am English and I do not fear for my life.

Annie Royle Taylor from *The Origin of the Tibetan Pioneer Mission*, 1894

Good God. When I consider the melancholy fate of so many of botany's votaries, I am tempted to ask whether men are in their right mind who so desperately risk life and everything else through the love of collecting plants.

Carl Linnaeus from *Glory of the Scientist*, 1737

Nobody but a person fond of Nat: history can imagine the pleasure of strolling under Cocoa nuts in a thicket of Bananas & Coffee plants, & an endless number of wild flowers — and this Island that has given me so much delight is reckoned the most uninteresting place.

Charles Darwin (1809–1882) in a letter to his father

Some friends have said 'You must have endured such hardship wandering in out-of-the-way corners of the earth'. I have. But such count for nothing, since I have lived in Nature's boundless halls and drank deeply of her pleasures … Where does hardship figure when the reward is such?

Ernest Henry Wilson (1876–1930) from *Plant Hunting* (1927)

Arriving was their passion.
Into the new place out of the blue
Flying, sailing, driving —
How well these veteran tourists knew
Each fashion of arriving.

Leaving a place behind them,
There was no sense of loss: they fed
Upon the act of leaving —
So hot their hearts for the land ahead —
As a kind of pre-conceiving.

Cecil Day Lewis (1904–1972) from 'The Tourists'

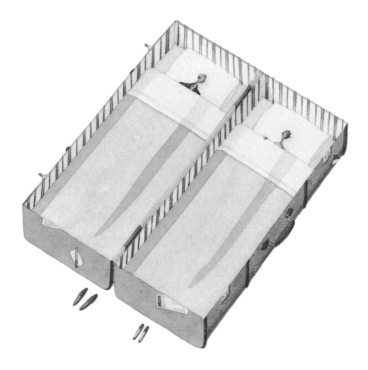

She went up the Nile as far as the first crocodile.

Samuel Butler (1835–1902)

Nothing surprises foreigners so much as the numbers of our countrymen that travel. The Swiss in particular often asked me how it happened, and said our country must be very unhealthy that everyone was so eager to get out of it.

William Bennett, writing from Abbeville-Montreuil in 1785

I suppose a little tour of Italy will be the next excursion; it furnishes rather an additional fund for elegant amusements in private life than anything useful.

Lord Findlater in a letter to a friend, 1768

A man who has not been in Italy is always conscious of an inferiority from his not having seen what it is expected a man should see.

Samuel Johnson (1709–1784) quoted in Boswell's *Life of Johnson*

Oh there is no Comparison between one's Sensations at home and those one feels at Naples.

Hester Piozzi, from *Observations and Reflections Made in the Course of a Journey through France, Italy and Germany*, 1789

I do not apprehend real advantages from seeing fine paintings and buildings can yet be of any advantage to you in the life you are like to lead hereafter and may … give you a taste of living beyond your circumstances.

John Mellish in a letter to his son, 15 April 1730

The pen refuses to describe the sufferings of some of the passengers during our smooth trip of ninety minutes: my own sensations were those of extreme surprise — it was not for that I paid my money.

Lewis Carroll (1832–1898) on crossing the English Channel

How many thousands and hundreds of thousands of English, with their mouths, eyes and purses wide open, have followed each other, in mournful succession, up and down the Rhine. . . .

Sir Francis Head from *The Brunnens of Nassau*, 1834

And is there then no earthly place
  Where we can rest, in dream Elysian,
Without some cursed, round English face,
  Popping up near, to break the vision?

Thomas Moore (1779–1852) from *Rhymes on the Road*

Mad dogs and Englishmen
Go out in the midday sun.

Noel Coward (1883–1973) from 'Mad Dogs and Englishmen'

The English of all people are the most provident upon these occasions, from a natural dread of being starved, which many of them are seized with the moment they lose sight of their native land — so that in the packets between Dover and Calais, or Ostend, it is no unusual thing to find as many fowls tongues, pastry and liquours as would victual a ship for a month's voyage.

Samuel Paterson from *Another Traveller!*, 1767

I encountered Mr Hackman, an Englishman, who has been walking the length and breadth of Europe for several years. I enquired of him what were his chief observations. He replied gruffly, 'I never look up,' and went on his way.

N Brooke, 1796

Diverse Discoveries

PART IV

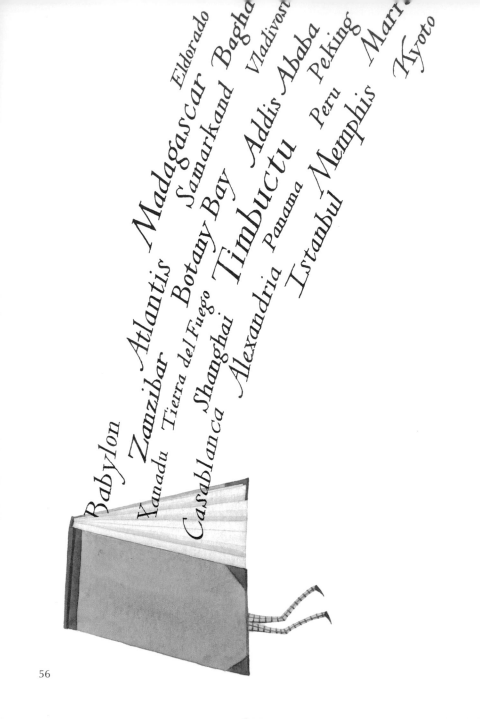

Babylon
Zanzibar
Atlantis
Xanadu Tierra delFuego
Madagascar
Samarkand
Botany Bay
Casablanca
Shanghai
Alexandria
Eldorado
Timbuctu
Panama
Addis Ababa
Baghd
Vladivost
Istanbul
Peru
Peking
Memphis
Marr
Kyoto

In travelling we visit names as well as places.

William Hazlitt (1778–1830) from *Notes of a Journey through France and Italy*

Countries, like people, are loved for their failings.

F Yeats Brown from *Bengal Lancer*, 1930

A place has almost a shyness of a person, with strangers; and its secret is not to be surprised by too direct interrogation.

Arthur Symons (1865–1945) from *Cities*

I once looked at a book called *A Record of the Islands and their Barbarians*, which recorded variations of season and of climate, and differences in topography and in peoples. I was surprised and said, 'How can there be such dissimilarities in the world?'

Cheng Ho, Chinese mariner, 1433

I may venture to pronounce the island a perfect garden.

Captain John Hunter from *An Historical Journal of the Transactions at Port Jackson and Norfolk Island,* May 1791

On my first landing everything was new to me, every Bird, every Insect, Flower &c. in short all was novelty around me, and was noticed with a degree of eager curiosity, and perturbation, that after a while subsided into calmness.

Elizabeth Macarthur in a letter from Australia, 1791

Some canoes came out to meet us … and invited us to follow them; but seeing as they were all armed I did not think fit to accept of their invitation.

Captain James Cook (1728–1779) from his own log and journals, 4 November 1769

At length we arrived safely at Timbuktu, just as the sun was
touching the horizon. I now saw this capital of Soudan, to reach
which had been so long the object of my wishes ... I experienced
an indescribable satisfaction. I never before felt a similar emotion
and my transport was extreme. I was obliged, however, to restrain
my feelings and to God alone did I confide my joy. How many
grateful thanksgivings did I pour forth for the protection which
God has vouchsafed to me, amidst obstacles and dangers which
appeared insurmountable.

This duty being ended, I looked around and found that the
sight before me, did not answer my expectations.

René Caillie from *Travels through Central Africa to Timbuktoo*

'Never, in the course of all my wanderings, had my eye rested on
a scene so dreary and inhospitable.'

Sir Joseph Hooker (1817–1911) *Himalayan Journals* 1849

Great God! This is an awful place.

Robert Falcon Scott (1868–1912) from his journal, 17 January 1912

I have nothing remarkable to say of the ascent. We soon got into a cloud, and never got out of it.

Anthony Trollope (1815–1882)

Never, never be such a fool as to go up a mountain ... Men still ascend eminences ... and descending, say they have been delighted. But it is a lie. They have been miserable the whole day.

W M Thackeray (1811–1863) from 'Wanderings of our Fat Contributor', *Punch*, 1844

The nasty, damp, dirty, slippery, boot-destroying, shin-breaking, veritable mountain! Let me recommend my friends to let it alone.

Anthony Trollope from *The West Indies and the Spanish Main*, 1859

No, I can't do with mountains at close quarters — they are always in the way, and they are so stupid, never moving and never doing anything but obtrude themselves.

D H Lawrence (1885–1930) in a letter to Lady Cynthia Asquith, 23 October 1913

I must go down to the seas, again, to the lonely sea and the sky,
And all I ask is a tall ship and a star to steer her by.

John Masefield (1878–1967) 'Sea Fever'

I wonder at the sea ... that vast Leviathan, rolled round the
earth, smiling in its sleep, waked into fury, fathomless, whither
goes it, is it of eternity or of nothing?

William Hazlitt (1778–1830) from *Notes of a Journey through France and
Italy*, 1821

Now would I give a thousand furlongs of sea for an acre of barren
ground — long heath, brown furze, anything. The wills above be
done, but I would fain die a dry death.

William Shakespeare (1564–1616) from *The Tempest*

He goes a great voyage that goes to the bottom of the sea.

H G Bohn, *Hand-book of Proverbs*, 1855

The difference between landscape and landscape is small, but there is a great difference between the beholders.

Ralph Waldo Emerson (1803–1882) from *Essays*, 1844

What's the Whim? Our whim will soon be, to go Naked, for you know, 'When we are at Rome &c.'

Dr George Worgan from *Journal of a Fleet Street Surgeon*, 1788

… myself to the best of my judgement plainly discerned that the women not copy our mother Eve even in the fig leaf.

Sir Joseph Banks (1743–1820) from *The Endeavour Journal of Joseph Banks*, 1768–1771

Our female porters were small and very strong in build, and, to enhance their attractions (we thought unsuccessfully), they covered their faces with black varnish.

Frank Kingdon-Ward (1885–1958)

The great ladies are arrayed in stuffs … they all wear drawers made of cotton cloth (and into the making of these some will put 60, 80, or even 100 ells of stuff). This they do to make themselves look large in the hips, for the men of those parts think that to be a great beauty in woman.

Marco Polo (1254–1324) from *The Book of Marco Polo the Venetian*

I ... have seen and gone through many diverse lands, and many provinces and kingdoms and isles ... where dwell many diverse folks, and of diverse manners and laws, and of diverse shapes of men.

Sir John Mandeville, *Travels*, c. 1360

[There] be ... folk that have but one foot, and they go so blyve [nimbly] that it is a marvel. And the foot is so large that it shadoweth all the body against the sun, when they will lie and rest them.

Sir John Mandeville, *Travels*

And in another isle be folk that go upon their hands and their feet as beasts. And they all be skinned and feathered, and they will leap as lightly into trees, and from tree to tree, as it were squirrels or apes.

Sir John Mandeville, *Travels*

To lie about a far country is easy.

Amharic proverb

The world, which is a curious sight
And very much unlike what people write.

Lord Byron (1788–1824) from 'Don Juan'

The manners of mankind do not differ so widely as our voyage
writers would make us believe. Perhaps it would be more
entertaining to add a few surprising customs of my own invention,
but nothing seems to me so agreeable as truth.

Lady Mary Wortley Montagu (1689–1762) from her *Letters*

Meditations on Travel

PART V

O how I long to travel back,
And tread again that ancient track!
That I might once more reach that plain,
Where first I left my glorious train;
From whence th'enlightened spirit sees
That shady city of palm-trees.

C J Vaughan (1816–1897) from 'The Retreat'

Travelling is almost like talking with men of other centuries.

Rene Descartes (1596–1650) from *Le Discours de la Methode*

Travellers always buy experience which no books can give.

Anonymous

When a traveller returneth home, let him not leave the countries
where he hath travelled altogether behind him.

Francis Bacon (1597–1625) from *Essays*

We carry within us wonders we seek without us.

Sir Thomas Browne (1605–1682)
from *Religio Medici*, 1643

A man travels the world over in search of what he needs
and returns home to find it.

George Moore (1852–1933) from *The Brook Kerith*

Take only memories. Leave nothing but footprints.

Chief Seattle

He who returns from a journey is not the same as he who left.

Chinese proverb

The real voyage of discovery is not in discovering new lands but in seeing with new eyes.

Marcel Proust (1871–1922)

I pity the man who can travel from Dan to Beersheba, and cry,
'tis all barren.

Laurence Sterne (1716–1788) from *A Sentimental Journey*

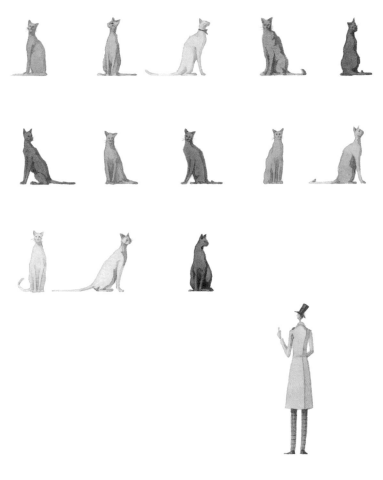

It is not worthwhile to go around the world to count the cats in Zanzibar.

Henry David Thoreau (1817–1862) in *Walden*, 1854

The great and recurrent question about abroad is, is it worth getting there?

Attributed to Rose Macaulay (1881–1958)

Abroad is utterly bloody.

Nancy Mitford (1904–1973) from *Love in a Cold Climate*

Hell stalks abroad.

Mary Wollstonecraft (1759–1797) from *Vindication of the Rights of Women*

So much travelling will put the mind to sleep.

Isabelle Eberhardt (1877–1904) from *The Passionate Nomad*

Too often travel, instead of broadening the mind, merely lengthens the conversation.

Elizabeth Drew in *The Literature of Gossip*, 1964

At my age travel broadens the behind.

Stephen Fry (b. 1957) in *The Liar*, 1991

I suggested that she take a trip around the world. 'Oh, I know,' returned the lady, yawning with ennui, 'but there's so many other places I want to see first.'

S J Perelman from *Westward Ha!*, 1948

The beckoning counts, and not the clicking of the latch behind you.

Freya Stark (1893–1993) in the *Sunday Telegraph*, 1993

For my part, I travel not to go anywhere, but to go. I travel for travel's sake. The great affair is to move.

Robert Louis Stevenson (1850–1894) from *Travels with a Donkey*

Among the therapeutic agents not to be found bottled up and labelled on our shelves, is Travelling; a means of prevention, of cure, and of restoration, which has been famous in all ages.

Daniel Drake, *Western Medical and Physical Journal*, 1827

The world is a very good world, but you must seek it; it will not do to neglect it.

Sydney Owenson, Lady Morgan (19th century)

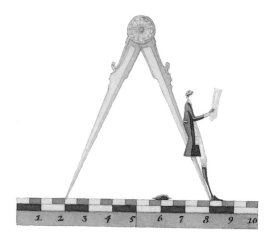

I can be bold to say that no man
will ever venture further than I have done.

Captain James Cook in his journals, January 1775

ACKNOWLEDGEMENTS

The compiler and Publisher would like to thank the
following for permission to use copyright material:
A & C Black (Publishers) Ltd for a quotation from
The Gentle Art of Tramping by Stephen Graham;
Peters, Fraser & Dunlop on behalf of the Estate of
S J Perelman for lines from *The Most of S J Perelman*
© S J Perelman; Pollinger Limited and the Estate of
Frieda Lawrence Ravagli for lines from a letter from
D H Lawrence © D H Lawrence 1913; The Random
House Group for lines from 'The Tourists' by C Day
Lewis from *The Complete Poems* by C Day Lewis,
published by Sinclair-Stevenson (1992), copyright
© 1992 in this edition, and the Estate of C Day
Lewis. Every endeavour has been made on the
part of the Publisher to contact copyright holders
not mentioned above and the Publisher will be
happy to include a full acknowledgement in any
future edition.